Morning's at Seven

ORDINARY TIMES IN
AN EXTRAORDINARY PLACE

Jonelle Fisher

Illustrated by Jenny Fisher

RABBIT HOUSE PRESS

Versailles, KY 40383

Copyright © 2001 by Jonelle Fisher
First Edition Published in the United States of America by St.
Crispian Press, 2001
Second Edition Published in the United States of America by
Rabbit House Press, July 2025

For inquiries about author appearances and/or volume
orders contact us at rabbithousepress.com.

ISBN 979-8-9929838-1-4

Edited by Erin Chandler

Cover and interior design; formatting: Daphne Vorel

This book is lovingly dedicated to

Jenny, Matt, Peter, Annie, Kim, and Kevin.

They have brought joy to my life

that is beyond measure.

Morning's at Seven

CONTENTS

Spring

Summer

Autumn

Winter

Forward

In the Summer of 1999, I was waiting to meet a friend at Joseph-Beth Booksellers when my eyes inadvertently fell on a small book that was on the table of the best sellers, *We Could Almost Eat Outside*, by Philippe Delerm, a Frenchman. I picked it up because that phrase is often used in our house. The line beneath the title on the cover, *An Appreciation of Life's Small Pleasures* charmed me enormously, and I sat right down on a bench there and read the eighty-three pages in its entirety. I bought all the copies that they had, planning to give them to our children and our friends.

Going home down the Old Frankfort Pike, I began to think of the small everyday things that are so special and wonderful for those of us fortunate enough to live in Woodford County, Kentucky. I decided it would be rewarding to record the memories of some of our own "small pleasures" and treasures before they are forgotten.

I also wanted to include just a few unique comments made by four small local children because of an innocence about them that brings joy to even the most dreary day.

These stories are centered around the years between 1950 and 1999. My greatest hope is that they will stir up even more happy memories.

Jonelle Fisher
Midway, Kentucky
August 28th, 2000

Morning's at Seven

The year's at the spring

And day's at the morn;

Morning's at seven;

The hill-side's dew-pearled

The lark's on the wing;

The snail's on the thorn:

God's in his heaven –

All's right with the world!

From "Pippa Passes"

By Robert Browning

Spring

"It was a very special day. Spring really is extraordinary as you grow older. The beginning all over again, much more than the beginning of the calendar year. You thank God for all the times you've seen it – felt it – and realized how short it all has seemed. Too few Springs when you count them all up. Fawn Leap's hill is bursting already with buttercups"

Personal Journal
March, 1982

Doggone Convertible

There is something special about riding in a convertible.

It has nothing to do with age or gender or position in the world. It has to do with heart. There are a lot of reasons why some people think it isn't such a great thing to do. They tell you that the sun beats down unmercifully in the heat of a summer's day. Your hair looks like a frizzled mop, especially if you have been riding in the back seat for any distance. If you are bald-headed the sun makes the top of your head almost blister any time you forget to wear a cap. In the winter it is very hard to get the heat up to comfortable. The music on the tape player is somewhat compromised by the inevitable noise of some part of the cloth top flapping. Also people for years have been saying that a convertible just isn't as safe as other cars. As a matter of fact, that was why the American car companies stopped making them during a short stint in the late 1970s. But when the lovers of the old ragtops kept buying the foreign models like hot cakes, the Americans decided to rethink their stand.

All of the above is true. However, wondrous balances step in here to describe many of the reasons why riding in a convertible is such an extraordinary thing. First of all, when you are in Woodford County, the scents that you experience as you ride along from early

3

March to late October are incredible: aromas of honeysuckle, catalpa tree blossoms, lilac, locus tree blossoms, clover, new mown hay, freshly cut tobacco and many more. Often you have to slow down to look for the origin, but if you look long enough, the fragrance will lead you right to it.

If the high school is planning a parade, you will be the first to be called to borrow your car for the Homecoming Queen and her court. This is true of county fairs as well. And even the Inaugural Parade for the Governor of Kentucky.

One of the most enjoyable things you can do in a convertible is to take your Labs to a pond at a friend's place in the country where the dogs can swim and walk around the perimeter of the water several times. Then you put the top down and drive the dogs home, making sure you take the long way back. You listen to Dwight Yoakum tapes as you cruise down the Aiken Road, The Old Frankfort Pike, and the Spring Station Road to Midway with the breeze drying off the dogs as you go.

But the best thing about riding in a convertible is when you put the top down for the first time on a spring night following a bitter cold winter, and ride through the countryside very slowly, dressed in wool sweaters, taking it all in. You aren't just driving through as you do in other cars. You are actually experiencing the scenery when the top is down and the air, the sights, scents, and sounds swirl in close around you. When you go gently down the long slope beside Waterford Farm, the temperature will drop at least ten degrees before warming up again as you climb the hill beside Fawn Leap. If you ride slowly with the top down at dusk around the Aiken Road near Sunny Slope Farm, you're sure to spot several deer near the road, and they have become so tame that they usually stand still and watch you with soulful eyes. If you stop the convertible, you feel a part of the deer's world as you gaze at each other for what seems to be an eternity.

Whether it is an attempt to feel young again, or to get an easy tan, or to look carefree as you glide by your friends who are driving in their Sports Utility Vehicles, there's just something about riding in a convertible.

SECOND CHRISTIAN CHURCH

Easter Parade

The Second Christian Church of Midway, said to be America's first organized African American Christian Church, was begun in the early 1800s. The present church was built in 1906. For years the women of the church prepared and served an Easter breakfast for those in town who would come after the Sunrise Service at the "Girl's School," or anyone else who happened to drop by. The congregation was small and the meal became an enormous responsibility for the few, but they endured for many years. They served bacon or sausage, grits, eggs, homemade biscuits, coffee, and orange juice. When an order was placed, it was then prepared in the basement of the church and sent up piping-hot on a dumb waiter that was hand operated to the area where the patrons were seated. That meal, costing two dollars and a half per plate, was the best you ever tasted.

Mister William Hamilton, a member of the church, would sit at the piano and play old songs during the entire morning. He had begun to play piano when he was about thirteen years old and had played a tuba or trumpet in his father's fifteen member marching band in Midway. He had known Cab Calloway, Louis Armstrong and Eubie Blake, but had not played with them. He had met Smoke Richardson in 1944 and played piano for his musical group for nineteen years, making the circuits of Columbus, Cincinnati, Cleveland, and New York City. In the course of his lifetime, he played for the Sunday Service of the Second Christian Church for over seventy years. He played at these Easter Breakfasts until after he was ninety. One of his favorite renditions, which he never failed to play on those wonderful mornings, was "Easter Parade." Old and young would gather around the piano and sing with him after they finished eating.

Of all memories of Easter, these mornings remain the most poignant.

The Big Guy

There is a beautiful little country church located in Woodford County that looks like a picture postcard. It is the Pisgah Presbyterian Church, founded in 1784. The graveyard there houses some of our earliest settlers, seven Revolutionary soldiers, and one of our past governors, Albert Benjamin (Happy) Chandler. Happy's great-grandson named Albert Benjamin IV in honor of the Governor (the next two generations) has been a member of the children's Sunday School class there since he was an infant. He is flanked on either side in his family by a sister (Lucie) who is older and a brother (Branham) who is younger. When Branham was born, Albert was told that he was now the big brother, and he should help protect his younger brother and was expected to be kind to him. Three-year-old Albert listened carefully.

At Sunday School on Easter morning, the teacher was telling the young children about Jesus and they were trying to understand all they were hearing. Finally the time ran out and the teacher told them they would talk about this wonderful story again on the next Sunday.

As the children gathered the next week in the beautiful little building behind the church, the teacher asked, "Who remembers the story we were talking about last Sunday? Who is the Big Guy we were learning about?"

Remembering how he had been entrusted to help little Branham because he was the bigger brother, Albert quickly raised his hand and answered proudly, "That would be me."

ALBERT CHANDLER IV

A Better Berry

There is a definite strawberry time, very short and sweet just from the end of May until about the official end of spring – but it produces the most delicious fruit this side of heaven. The Kentucky Berry is usually smaller than its California cousin, but it makes up for what it lacks in size by its unique flavor. Before Strawberries were shipped from state to state, they were not eaten locally except during these very special weeks. The rest of the year was spent yearning for the first taste of the bountiful red berries. In today's world there are very few days in your life when you can't find strawberries in any big grocery story in any state, thanks to modern shipping. This consistent availability has dulled the excitement of the anticipation, and the waiting has lessened the craving in direct proportion. They tasted better when they were looked upon as a four-week gastronomical wonder.

In Woodford County there are two orchards that have berry patches where the public may come pick once the crop comes in: Garrett's Orchard on Shannon Run Road and Kaenzig's Orchard on the Pinckard Pike. These two operations are just a couple of miles apart and are both a real asset to the county. A few people have patches in their own gardens, and sometimes you're invited to come pick there. Almost everywhere you go to eat around here during this time, your dessert will feature strawberries.

To enjoy the fun of picking the berries, you have to arrive very early in the morning as soon as the orchard is open, to get a good spot. Serious pickers who come to gather enough to freeze for the family for the winter will station themselves between the heads of two rows and will move in a professional way, quickly gathering the crop from both sides as they go. Usually there will be a white stick standing at the head of a row that has not been freshly picked. After you pluck those strawberries, you are asked to move the stick to the place where you stopped, so the next person will know just where to start looking for an unspoiled area. Then he will move the stick when he finishes as well.

People will be talking and laughing freely to the folks around them that they hardly know. There is quite a fellowship in the talk of the berry pickers, because most are excited and happy to be there another year, gleaning the beautiful, delicious berry from its hiding place under the straw. (There is always straw placed around each plant in a well-defined patch, and you have to wonder if that had anything to do with the name being "straw" berry. Veteran growers are convinced that the straw is used to keep down weeds and as a mulch – and that it has nothing to do with the name as far as they know.)

Realizing when to quit is the real challenge of picking strawberries. As sure as you make up your mind that the next plant will be your last, you will see gleaming red peeking out in many different directions under the dew-dampened green leaves down the row, and you know you simply must do "one more" plant. It never fails to happen. You pick more than you could ever use yourself, even counting the berries that you drop in a freezer bag after removing the green stems. You divide some of the rest up in several small baskets and decide to take them to older people in Midway who can no longer pick for themselves, and to those friends who do not have the time to go to the orchards. People are so appreciative of freshly picked Kentucky strawberries that you go home pretty pleased with your morning. It is now time to sit down to a bowl of fresh ones yourself, adding just a little bit of vanilla ice cream on top. Ahhh. Life is good.

TOM BOMBADIL

The Encounter

Among life's most wonderful creatures is the Golden Retriever dog. This breed is consistently loyal, friendly, intelligent, and beautiful. Our family was lucky enough to own one for the eleven years of his life. We named him Tom Bombadil for the character in Tolkien's *Lord of the Rings*. He had only one trick – he would shake "hands" with anyone who came to see us.

One bitter cold winter morning when he was about five years old, I dressed warmly and went out in the snow to play with Tom for about twenty minutes. He chased sticks, rolled in the snow, ran after me, barked at the neighbors, and had a wonderful time. I was exhausted by all the exercise in the cold and came inside. As I was taking off my boots, he scratched loudly at the door. I opened it for him to come in, but he backed away and just looked at me with those large trusting eyes. He was asking me to come out again to play as clearly as if he were speaking. I put my boots back on.

The next Spring, Tom and I went to the top field at Fawn Leap Farm where we were allowed to take our daily stroll. He was running ahead of me when I saw him stop and grow rigid with his tail pointed up and stiff – but he was not barking. He was peering across the plank fence at a beautiful red fox. They were intensely staring at each other from about thirty feet. The fox was the same color as Tom, but half as large with a lovely, pointed face and huge red tail. They were standing dead still. When I called to Tom he came running, glad to get out of a confrontation. I guess there were cubs nearby, and the mother was protecting them as best she could. When we left, I saw her sauntering off across the green fields.

The Play's the Thing

The Midway Lions Club has been an outstanding organization since its inception in 1945. Besides its active participation in its wonderful eye-glass project, the Club contributes generously to every town function, operates a snack bar at Midway's annual Railroad Days, provides American and Kentucky flags to be flown at all three cemeteries in the town, and gives baskets of food to the needy every Christmas. The Lions host a Ladies' Night every October where the ladies are honored, the members are recognized for their efforts during the year, and entertainment is provided. This compellation is just a smattering of what they do, the list could go on and on ad infinitum.

In 1952 and again in 1954 they decided to give a play. They asked "Miss Amanda" Hicks to direct it and they used local talent. For the 1952 presentation, they chose "Gold in the Hills," subtitled "The Dead Sister's Secret." In 1954 it was to be "The Curse of an Aching Heart" or "Caught in the Spider's Web." Both plays turned out to be enormous hits.

"Gold in the Hills" was a Gay Nineties melodrama, complete with a villain, a young damsel and a hero. The three "stars" were Jack Reilly, Fannie Jean Pruitt and Jesse Ward. However, half the town ended up taking roles as they all wanted to be part of the fun. Some of the other characters were played by Mrs. John Johnson, Steele Davis, Miss Maxine House, Joe Hancock, Frank and Sonny Sonderman, Phil Weisenberger, Mister and Mrs. Stan Gajdik, Bob Hicks, John Wehrle, L. M. Pruitt, James Raisor, Richard Starks and Dr. Ben Roach. Colonel Bill Buster was the Master of Ceremonies. Dr. Roach and his barbershop quartet used the second act as an excuse to sing, as the scene was set in a barroom. The quartet was made with Ben as lead tenor, John T. Mitchell as tenor, Warren Mitchell as baritone and Karl Jefferson as bass.

The play was first given at the Midway Public School auditorium in April and there was standing room only. The action had to be stopped at many intervals because of a loud hissing and booing from the delighted audience. At one point the villain (Jack Reilly) forgot his lines but he recovered nicely by frantically looking out at the audience and exclaiming, "Curses!! My line doth elude me!!" and he reached into his hip pocket and whipped out a script book to look up his lines. This quick thinking brought down the house and that was the one line that no one ever forgot.

That play was considered such a success that the Versailles Kiwanis, Rotary and Barbershop Clubs asked that it be brought to Versailles for the "Woodford Follies of 1952" at the Versailles High School Auditorium in May. Tickets were a dollar for adults and fifty cents for children, with all proceeds going to benefit the Woodford Memorial Hospital.

Two years later, "The Curse of an Aching Heart" was given and was also an enormous success. "Miss Amanda" directed once again and the leading roles were played by Janna Reed, Jesse Ward, Frank Sonderman, Mrs. Paul Noel, Mrs. O.B. Wilder, Mrs. Rupert Breeden, Mrs. James Raisor, Bill Buster, and others. A review in the Woodford Sun of February, 1954, gave an insight into the play: "A half score and more terrestrial beings seek a solution to the dastard deviltry of a demonic individual whose actions are super saturated with sanctimonious signs of so-called shenanigans."

The meeting of the Lions Club following the production was a dinner celebration, and the president presented "Miss Amanda" with a gift of appreciation.

One footnote about the plays – in 1952, two local young people, Fannie Jean Pruitt and Joe Hancock were introduced to one another at play practice, fell in love and married. Stories just don't end any better than that.

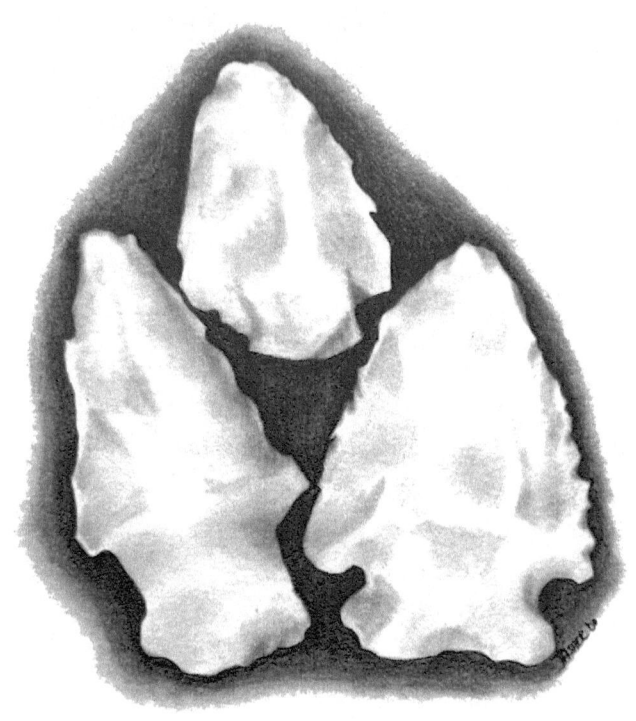

Arrowheads

Historians have reason to believe that centuries ago the Adena Indians lived around what would eventually become Woodford County. They came because of the abundance of water in creeks, springs and branches, and because of the bountiful hunting grounds this area afforded them. As proof of their existence, they left behind enormous Indian burial mounds on what is now Adena Springs Farm located on the Versailles-Frankfort Road, and on Sunny Slope Farm on the Aiken Road.

It is thought that several Indian tribes inhabited land or at least hunted around here later on, before the pioneers came in the eighteenth century. They left behind scores of their arrowheads and pieces of their tools which can still be found hidden down under the surface of the ground. The tribes that are thought to have been in Kentucky include the Cherokee, the Delaware, the Iroquois, and the Shawnee. One can only imagine what they thought when they first discovered the powerful stream of water gushing out where Adena Springs is located today. That source still produces from seven hundred to one thousand gallons of water per minute, enough to supply the city of Versailles if necessary. If you lie down on the concrete structure that has been built over the spring to protect the waters, you can witness the enormous flow that runs continuously down to the branch. The water is startlingly cold.

Woodford County natives continue to look for arrowheads and other Indian artifacts. In the twenty years that Dick Starks farmed Stonewall Farm, he picked up about five hundred pieces of artifacts on that land. Later on when he retired, he mounted his best (read that "perfect") arrowheads on wooden boards covered with red and green velvet and displayed them in his house over his desk. His collection has been said to be even better than that of former President Lyndon Johnson. Dick will tell you that the best time to look for arrowheads is in the spring after a rain in a freshly plowed field.

If you find a perfect arrowhead you will likely realize that the elation of discovery overshadows the joy of possessing that small, incredible piece of Kentucky's past. Somehow in your mind, the true ownership will always belong to the craftsman. You think just how difficult it would have been to cut it out by hand, and how disconcerting it would have been to have used it just once and not been able to find it to use again. If you rub your fingers over the surface and along the still sharp edge of arrowheads, you stand in awe as visions of the hands that first held them come to you.

Asparagus

At the time when Pin Oak Farm was located at the corner of US 60 and the Midway-Versailles Pike, it extended a great length down both roads, as it contained a large acreage. The owner kept the grounds immaculate, and people would pull their cars off to the side of the Midway Pike to get out and look at the Simmental cattle or to make photographs of the breathtaking scenery that was commonplace on the farm in almost any direction. The man in charge of keeping the white plank fences repaired and painted said that it was a year-round job – once he and his crew finished refurbishing the miles of fencerows, it was time to start over again at the beginning. It was a never-ending job done to perfection.

But there was another factor about Pin Oak Farm that made it even more extraordinary. From mid-April until the Derby, a plain board sign would appear almost daily at the Midway Road entrance to the farm. It would have the word "ASPARAGUS" painted roughly on it in white, with an arrow indicating the way back to a certain barn. It was the most delicious asparagus in the world, and many locals would make the trek out to the barn every single morning that the sign was up, knowing the season would not last long. They did not want to miss such an opportunity even for a day.

ASPARAGUS

The people who worked on the farm would harvest the asparagus early every morning, (but if you went too early, you would have to wait for the truck to come in with the morning's bounty), weigh it and put it in pound bundles. The asparagus would be graded from the thicker stalk to the thinner, and buyers could choose which size they preferred. It was so fresh that small clumps of soil would still be clinging to the stalks. If you were giving a huge party, perhaps on Derby Day, you could call several days ahead to reserve enough to serve. Your order would be bagged and waiting when you came to pick it up. Josephine Abercrombie, the owner of Pin Oak Farm, had generously handed over the asparagus project to the farm workers. It was theirs to tend, to harvest, and to sell, with the profits being theirs to keep at the end of the season. It was truly a wonderful set up.

Once when we were going to visit our family in Darien, Connecticut, our plane left from the Lexington airport around eleven in the morning. We put about three inches of ice in an old ice bucket and closed the lid tightly. On the way to the airport, we detoured by the Pin Oak Farm. We asked the ladies to fill the ice bucket completely with asparagus, and to please cut the stalks so they would stand straight up in the bucket with the lid on tight. They loved the idea that their crop was on its way to Connecticut, and they gave us the best they had to offer that morning. We hand-carried the bucket on the plane, hoping the flight attendant wouldn't object.

MORNING'S AT SEVEN

That evening my sister and her husband gave a party for us. She steamed the asparagus at the last minute, serving it with just a trace of salt and lemon. The rest of her menu went virtually unnoticed as every guest there raved and raved over the fresh asparagus. They swore it must be a different variety than any they had ever eaten before, as they had never tasted anything that delicious. It was devoured in the wink of an eye. The party was a smashing success, primarily due to the airlifted fresh asparagus.

May Day

There is a college for girls at Midway with a long and interesting history. It was first a school for orphans, founded by Dr. L. L. Pinkerton and opening in 1849. At one point it was a school for seventh through twelfth graders; then a junior college was added. Later the high school was phased out and the school became Midway College. As time progressed the school has remained a star in the crown of the town, and through the years it has presented the locals with several perks that they would not have otherwise had.

The public was invited to plays put on by the school Drama Club and programs by well-known celebrities. The town was on the invitation list for each year's graduation exercises, usually held at the amphitheater.

At one time, the school had many foreign students and once a year they would prepare a dinner with exotic foods of their countries. These would be presented to the public with great pride, and the men and women of the community would flock to taste the unusual fare.

During two or three summers the Woodford County Theatrical Arts Association leased the amphitheater and gave memorable outdoor productions of popular Broadway hits. Plays such as Mame, The Fantasticks, and Little Shop of Horrors were directed and performed by local county talent on four evenings a week for about six weeks each summer. When they were "sold out," as they often were, a number of young people would come and sit on the hillside, humming the songs along with the cast. The sound of the music could be heard all over the town while each play was going on, to the delight of folks sitting on their porches at home.

The "May Day" celebrations were some of the most memorable programs of the school. Held on the afternoons following the Board of Trustees' meeting in May, they were beautifully done each year. In the 1950s and early 1960s, the programs were directed by Margaret Ware Parrish, who left no stone unturned. She and the girls worked endlessly on each production all semester long, planning a theme and gathering costumes and props.

The May Queen would be presented along with her Maid of Honor, a Spirit of Midway Junior College and a Spirit of Pinkerton High School. The girls from the senior class would be in pastel dresses, and they would form an aisle for the queen and her attendants. The queen always wore a white dress and a cape with a long train. The train would be carried by two little girls, either relatives of the college personnel or garnered from the town. Then the seniors would walk down to the stage where a young boy would be standing to help them up the few stairs onto the stage of the amphitheater. There they would sit and watch the show that had been honed to perfection by Margaret Ware and the girls of the other classes.

Some programs of that era were named, "Musical Memories," "Americana," "Best of Broadway," and "American Heritage." The props included sparklers, flags, and fireworks. The celebrations always included a beautiful dance around the May pole. Margaret Ware remembers once when the girls helped her put chicken wire across the top of the back of the amphitheater. Then they made hundreds of paper wisteria blossoms to hang on the wire. Early in the morning of the presentation they picked just enough greenery to mix with the wisteria so it would look fresh, and it held up through the program for the Board.

Sadly, the custom of May Day has been abandoned. Nowadays, most college girls would consider themselves a little too sophisticated to be dancing around a May pole on a beautiful May afternoon on a lovely hill that is covered with memories of the days of white dresses and wisteria.

Summer

"Tonight was the last night before school starts for Matt and Jenny. This summer has been the best and we have enjoyed being with the children more than ever. As I was helping them get ready for bed, they were talking excitedly about who their teachers would be and who would be on their bus in the morning. They were happy and anxious to start another year. At that moment, I could hear the gentle bell of the ice cream truck over on Winter Street making its last appeal, ringing out the end of summer. It was sad for me that the children didn't even hear it."

Personal Journal
August, 1965

BEN ROACH AT BAT

Bases Loaded

The old Midway Public School, now a lovely apartment complex restored to look just like it did when it was built in 1924, has been the scene of many happy occasions. When it was still a school, there were activities all year long, and most of the town would take advantage of the entertainment.

First in the school year, there would be the Halloween party where there would be Pin the Tail on the Donkey, bobbing for apples, prettiest, ugliest, and most original costume awards, a doll show, a puppet show, a cake walk, other games and treats. Later on at school basketball games spectators would sit on a balcony which hung out almost over part of the court. And sometimes the whole structure would shake from the cheering and jumping up and down of the fans. The highlight of Midway's basketball fame came in 1937 when the team won the Kentucky State Championship. The town will never forget the pride they felt over this accomplishment.

The building then had a marvelous auditorium with surprisingly good acoustics, where you could go in December to see the Christmas play. This auditorium was also used when there arose a need for a town meeting, or for a Lion's Club, or Women's Club affair.

In the spring there would be junior and senior plays at the school and then graduation. (The school was a high school until the early 1950s when it was declared that it would be beneficial for the students all over the country to go to one combined school, and, of course, that school would be located in Versailles. There was a huge separation of opinion on the worth of this idea, but it was passed by the School Board, and Midway lost its top grades.)

At the school, the summertime activities were among the best. The Summer Recreation Program allowed time for Little League, Pony League, softball and baseball, tennis, badminton, croquet, volleyball, and crafts. There were activities going on from two o'clock to five Monday through Friday, and several evenings. In its heyday there were four Little League teams and six slow pitch adult teams. The adult teams were sponsored by the Baptist Church, Mount Vernon Church, the Christian Church, SCAME, The Methodist Church, the College of the Bible. All summer long there would be huge crowds gathered on the hillside for each and every game.

One of the big attractions for the crowds at the men's games was Mister Clay Guy, who was the umpire for every important game year after year. He was a fairly short man, but with a stocky frame and a full-blown knowledge about how to call a ball. No matter how many games were played in an evening, Clay was expected to stay for them all and carry out his duty. No one remembers a single time that an opinion of his was ever questioned by either side in all the games he officiated at Midway ball field. When he spoke at a ball game, everybody listened because his voice of authority was trusted to get it right.

Once when Bill Clark's son was active in the Little League program, Bill realized that the place had no concession stand. By pure chance, Mary Fisher, a friend to Bill and owner of the renowned Dixiana Farm, mentioned that she had a very large chicken house that she no longer wanted. Bill asked if he might come and get it for the ballpark. She was pleased to let it go. Bill then got a friend who owned a bulldozer slide to go to Dixiana with him where they jacked up the twenty-four foot building and brought it down to the ballfield. They left the backdoor like it was but cut two big panels out with a power saw. They put little chains on these panels and there was the concession stand. And thus, it happened that the first snack bar at the Midway Recreation Program was Mary Fisher's chicken house.

For several years Midway had a formidable Little League because boys would come from all around to play here. Now a rule has been passed that children must represent their own community.

One of the best coaches for the Little League teams was Mr. Sam Fisher. If a child showed up for practice and put forth any effort at all, Mr. Sam let him play at least one inning in the weekly game, no matter how poorly he played. Winning wasn't as important to Mr. Sam as being fair to the children. Mothers and friends would walk out to the old school, taking the younger children to play on the playground swings and slides, while they watched the older children bat the ball and run around the bases. Many afternoons were whiled away just sitting on the grassy knoll enjoying your neighbors and the day.

Back in the 1960s, some of the mens' teams took their game very seriously. Everybody who was there one night will remember the eyeball-to-eyeball confrontation between the doctor and the minister that was finally settled without blows because of the intervention of some teammates. All the men played to WIN, and there were some really good players that the whole town would turn out to watch.

The best time of all would be when the games ran very late and most of the onlookers would have given up and gone home. The sounds of the bat hitting the ball and the cheering from the stout hearted who were still watching would drift over the entire town through the opened summer windows lulling us all to sleep.

Mulligan's Stew

There was a golden age in Midway during the late 1950s and early 1960s before the interstate opened up an exit, and before air conditioners and television sets took most people inside their homes in the evenings. At that time, you could call by name everyone who lived on your entire street. You could sit on your porch and speak to neighbors as they took walks after supper to cool off. Most of the time these friends would stop to visit a while. News would be shared; crops, weather and politics would be thoroughly discussed. Even if there was no one sitting on a porch you wouldn't mind calling through a screen door if you wanted to talk. But it's different to knock at a closed front door that is keeping the cool air conditioning inside your neighbor's house. To knock would make you feel like you were intruding.

Sometimes neighbors would walk over to visit after supper and the children would be ready to give a "show" written, directed, produced, and performed by several of the neighborhood children. The "stage" would be a patio with lawn chairs set up on the grass for the parents and their visitors. There would be written "rules" for the guests who would have paid a nickel to see the show. This list of rules would be handed out as tickets, and once when it was to be a tumbling show there were these three regulations listed:

37

1. Say nothing (while) during the show.

2. Stay in your seats.

3. Don't get on the matrus.

If you happen to walk downtown to the drugstore around lunchtime, you would see Lucy Bethel Holt, who was a town character, sitting at the counter of the Bit and Spur Café, eating her grilled tomato and cheese sandwich and sipping on her Coca Cola. Children would be sitting near her on high stools eating ice cream cones while they waited for their mother to have a prescription filled on the "other side" of the drugstore.

This was an era when mothers would sit in each other's backyards for an entire afternoon, watching their children play together, while they sipped a cup of tea or a glass of lemonade and talked.

One of our closet neighbors was "Miss Amanda" Hicks, who lived in a wonderful log cabin in the side yard of our house. She was special to each of our children, but particularly kind to our son Matt. Her grandson R. W. was the same age as Matt and his best friend. Many times Matt was included for over-nights spent with "Granny" where frequently he and R. W. would be allowed to cook supper. During the summer after their fourth grade, Miss Amanda decided to teach the two boys how to type. Every day she drove them to her

official class until they reached sixty hours, and she issued a report card at the end of the session.

But the thing Matt enjoyed the most with Miss Amanda was the cooking as he just wasn't allowed to do that at home. When he was eight years old, he came in our kitchen one morning early after having spent the night at Miss Amanda's. He handed three "Resapies" to me copied carefully in his own handwriting, using his own spelling. Two were for cookies and one was for Mulligan's Stew. The stew is recorded below exactly as it appeared.

MULLIGAN'S STEW

Melt 1 TABLESPOON SHORTNING

ADD 1 pound beef cut into small Peises

BROWN OVER medium heat

ADD 1 teaspoon salt

1 can tomato soup (10 ½ oz)

2 soup cans water

Cover tightly and let cool slowley until tender about 1 hr.

ADD 3 carrets

3 potatos cut into 4 peises

2 onions cut into 4 peises

Cover and cooking slowley about thirty minuts.

I have often remembered the days (and nights) that Matt spent with Miss Amanda and thought of the comparison of his childhood and education with those of children of today, thirty-five years later. I know there have been vast improvements in the classroom, and I understand that children of today know all about the computer, the Internet, and the Web. All this has enormously changed the world in which they live and has made more information available to them at an earlier age than we (or Matt) ever dreamed of. But I also have to wonder how many of these more sophisticated, more mature, and better educated children of today would have any idea of how to come up with a good Mulligan's Stew.

The Fourth of July

Once upon a time there were about sixty friends in and around Midway who would celebrate holidays and special days together. Each couple would be host when it was their turn and the friends would come, bringing food and drink. The critical celebrations were Derby Day, house warmings, and New Year's Eve. House warmings were fun because of the elaborate ruses that were created to make the evening a surprise for the hapless couple who had just moved into a new house. At all these outings there was never entertainment planned – the friends just wanted to socialize with their neighbors, enjoy each other's company and find out "the news" of the community.

In the mid-1950s Bob and Niesje Hicks reached the age when the annual dues to the Country Club in Lexington where they belonged nearly doubled, and this made them begin to think seriously whether they used this facility enough to justify such steep membership fees. But their entire family loved to swim, and they didn't want to deny that pleasure. So, they settled this dilemma by building a good-sized swimming pool in their side yard where they lived in the country. It was the first such pool in the community, and their friends watched the digging with awe and curiosity.

THE FOURTH OF JULY

It turned out to be a perfect solution to their problem. With a pool in the yard, Bob would swim every evening after a hard day of working on the farm and Neisje and the two girls would swim laps daily for their exercise. They were incredibly generous sharing these pleasures with their friends, and soon families from town flocked to the pool on hot summer days. Many Midway children learned how to swim in that pool. It became a meeting place for friends to gather as soon as they could get the chores of the day out of the way.

When the pool was about a year old, Bob and Niesje decided to start a tradition of inviting their circle of friends and the friends' children out to celebrate the Fourth of July every year. The suggested time for arrival was about four o'clock in the afternoon. Everyone would be expected to bring one dish and their family's meat and drink, and all the food would be placed on the big table between the house and the pool. Sometimes Bob would heat up the big old grill and cook hamburgers or steaks while the children ran around chasing each other, diving in and getting out of the pool a thousand times and squealing with delight. There would always be one man or two in the water to act as referees to keep the children safe.

After swimming for a couple of hours the children would finally get out of the water long enough to dry off for the picnic, which would be devoured in just a few minutes. Then the begging would start because the youngsters would want to swim for just a few minutes more. After the appropriate time elapsed, parents usually relented, and the kids jumped in for another round.

If we were lucky, someone would have brought fireworks and sparklers, and this would be the icing on the cake of the perfect day. After the long strenuous afternoon, the children would usually be asleep in the car before it turned in the driveway of home that evening.

Those magical annual Fourth of July get-togethers became cherished as one of the favorite celebrations of the year for children and grownups alike. Just like Camelot, it seemed it never rained til after sundown on any Fourth of July at the Hick's pool.

RICHARD

Richard

Along the entire southern border of our property, there grows a tall winter honeysuckle hedge. The nursery man who delivered the seventy plants declared that winter honeysuckle never needs trimming and that it grows to about six feet high. I'm reminded of his erroneous theory three times each summer when I take my trusty pocketknife and cut back the enormous, prickly branches so they will not scratch our neighbor's car as he drives up his driveway in the afternoons. I like to use a pocketknife and do one branch at a time even though it takes a lot longer because this method of pruning makes the plant look natural and flowing. The entire effort takes about six hours to complete and by the time I finish, I realize this is the kind of job that makes you humble. This is especially true if you fail to recognize the several vines of poison ivy neatly tucked in between tight places in the hedge, making you unaware of them until it's too late and you have pulled them out with your bare hands.

Our neighbors on the other side of the hedge are Jim and Marsha Starks and their children, Elizabeth, Richard, and Will. The children are good kids and Jack and I enjoy them enormously.

Richard has always been a sensitive child, tall for his age, and he has blonde hair cut very short. He has fair skin with dimples in his cheeks, and blue eyes. When he was small, he would come and sit and talk to me in the summers when he would see me reading in my yard. This was a joy to me as Richard was inevitably entertaining and usually had a good story to tell. One day when I was desperately sad because of a family tragedy, three-year-old Richard came to sit with me. When I did not respond to his talking with my usual enthusiasm, he asked if he might sing a song that he had learned at Sunday School to try to make me happy. I said of course, and he began to sing "My King Rides on a Donkey." It was like a tonic for me, and it helped me more than I would have thought possible.

At another time, Elizabeth had been ill for a couple of days and Jack went over to give her a shot to make her well. Richard cried as hard as Elizabeth because he didn't want to see her hurt, then called out goodbye to Jack when he left, running from one window to the next, calling again and again to be sure Jack knew he wasn't mad at him.

In the late summer of 1992 when Richard was four, we were going on a trip that would last for ten days, and I needed to cut the hedge before we left. It was in the afternoon when I started, and I knew I had to hurry to get it done before dark. Once started, there was no turning back and I was clipping away as fast as I could. After a while Richard came out to his driveway and talked to me as I clipped. His childish prattle made the time pass quickly for me as I worked.

MORNING'S AT SEVEN

When the sun was sinking and I was still concentrating on my clipping, all of a sudden, Richard stopped talking. He was staring with those big blue eyes standing motionless and listening. I asked if there was anything wrong, and he answered, "I hear night comin'." Startled, I stopped clipping and asked what he had said. "Listen," he repeated, "you can hear night comin'." I listened intently and the summer night sounds of crickets, katydids, and cicadas were everywhere. I had been too busy and preoccupied to hear their message. It was a very special moment for me, and I was sorry when he called, "Goodbye Mrs. Fisher" and turned to run inside.

"Awesome in Magnitude"

Three times during the past twenty-five years the Lions Club has sponsored a circus to come to Midway for the town's entertainment and to make money for their community services. Nothing in the world could be more exciting for old and young in this small community than to have a circus arrive with all of its paraphernalia. Children would run wide-eyed to watch the elephant pull the ropes up for the center pole of the tent and the setting up of the other acts. There would be two performances per circus, and both would garner an enormous crowd. Most children would beg to stay and see the acts twice.

When a circus would want to come to town, the owner would contact the Lions Club with an offer of a percentage of the money that would be taken in on admission tickets. The Club's duties were to find a location and to provide hay and water for the animals. The rest would be taken care of by the circus people. If the deal sounded good, the Club would sponsor the circus and would benefit by taking an active part in selling the tickets. Usually, the advanced tickets would be considerably cheaper than those purchased at the gate.

In July of 1975 the Fisher Brothers Circus arrived at the Midway ballpark with clowns, elephants, acrobats, and trained animals. Steele Davis and Bill Clark went to Lexington to procure the peanuts and popcorn to sell during the performances, as the Lions Club would take all the money from the sale of these treats.

In June of 1977, the American Big Top Wild Animal Circus was held in the "courtyard" of the Midway Elementary School, and it is remembered that this one had a fat lady, a snake, and a goat act in addition to the usual fair.

The last circus that came to town was called The King Royal Big Top Circus and it was held at the Midway City Park. The ad claimed it was "Awesome in Magnitude," and that there would be one hundred minutes of thrills and laughs in each performance. Lion Nelson Prewitt related later that this particular circus would not be coming to town again as the elephant that was necessary to raise the pole had been hit by lightning and had passed away in Florida.

At the circus performance in 1975, a girl, her husband, and her father, would ride horses around the tent, doing tricks as they rode bareback. During one of these shows, the girl fell from her horse and requested to be seen by the doctor who was in the crowd. Her husband brought her down to the doctor's office right away. As it turned out, she was eight months pregnant and was afraid the fall would start her labor. The doctor explained later, "She was a pretty girl. Her father was an alcoholic, and I think that he had fallen off the horse a time or two. She said she needed to be near to him to help in any way she could. She was trying to follow in the footsteps of the family in bareback riding. Can you imagine that? It's amazing that you have these nice people – you wonder how they ever got involved in working in a small circus. You know they barely make a living. But obviously it was their life, and they loved it. It was all they wanted to do, maybe it was all they could do. I don't know. She was not in labor, and they went back to the circus."

She was a lovely girl, and the doctor regretted the hardships of the life she was leading. The circus left town the next morning early and the girl went on her way, but she had left a lasting impression of grace and dignity with the doctor.

RAY HARM, MATT, JENNY AND PETER

The Kentucky

The Kentucky River, which borders Woodford County for several miles to the south and to the west, provides water for our daily use and our pure enjoyment. One of the most beautiful rivers in the country, it has a long and fascinating history. Thankfully, the natural beauty of it has been preserved in numerous paintings by the renowned artist Paul Sawyier.

There was a time in the life of our family when our favorite outings were to the Kentucky where we had a small runabout boat. These treks made perfect "getaways" for my hurried General Practitioner husband Jack. We rented space at the dock at Clifton for the spring, summer and autumn months every year, usually going down there until the winter turned too cold, around Thanksgiving.

The favorite time of year on the river for Jack and me was in the fall when it was quiet from most other motorboats, and you could drift and read a good book in the cool afternoon. We could motor upstream, with plans to drift back to Clifton if necessary because we were never positive that the old motor would start up again. We didn't want to have to paddle upstream to get home.

The children loved the summer best when we would go down for the day with picnic lunches, life preservers and buckets with shovels. Just a few curves down from Clifton on the Anderson County side of the river was a small sandy spot where we could spread out. Someone who had found the spot before us had climbed a tree on the bank and tied a thick rope around a limb that hung out over the river. The children could grab onto it, climb back up on the bank, take a running leap and swing out over the water to drop in. They never tired of this activity. All four learned to waterski, and this really added to the enjoyment. Jack took our two boys and a couple of their friends down to the sandy spot for an overnight stay several times, swearing each time when he got home that he would never do that again. However, sleeping on the bank of the Kentucky River was the price you had to pay to be able to look up at the moon and stars out over the tranquil water. This always lured him back again.

Another significant part of our enjoyment of the Kentucky was the 1966 opening of the "Buckley Wildlife Sanctuary," built on a bluff overlooking the river. There were three trails through the woods which were designated by different colors of paint on the trunks of trees growing along the paths. The children would run ahead trying to be the first to find the color markings that told us we were still on the trail. The "white" pathway led to where you could see the river down below and this was the favorite. Mr. Elwood Carr, who was the caretaker would give delightful lectures, and the children would listen in wonder. When he told of eating a little bit of a poison ivy leaf every morning until he conquered his allergy, they were in awe of this man. We also learned which wild plant we could chew on safely to stave off thirst when we were lost in the woods. Our son Peter tested that knowledge every time we went on walks for a long time after that.

Once there was a large turnout when the well-known artist and naturalist Ray Harm came to lecture. He stood on the lawn in front of the house that was named for him to give his talk. He had brought a baby possum which he had hanging on his arm by its long, skinny tail. If a bird whistled while he was talking, he would immediately identify it by its call.

Jack and I give much credit to the Kentucky River and its environs for the concerned attitude our grown children now have about the preservation of our natural beauty, land, and water. We are most truly grateful for that.

Primroses in July

Margaret Ware Parrish, a wonderful lady who lives on a farm outside of the town of Midway, takes care of and feeds all the stray cats in town – even paying their vet fees when the need arises. She feeds the wild ducks that come to the pond in the winter, organizes town celebrations with regularity, keeps historical records for Midway, flies a beautiful array of treasured kites when the winds permit, and grows a prolific bed of Evening Primroses.

Around the first week of July, Margaret Ware calls her friends with a jubilant, "The primroses are blooming! Come see!" And everyone who has ever seen these flowers bloom get immediately in a car and races out to be among the first to witness this delight of summer.

The Evening Primroses are so unusual they defy descriptions. About nine o'clock in the evening when the sun has begun to get low and no longer shines on the primroses, they start to move. The blossoms on the long stems begin to twist a little, then turn, then spin, and POP open while you watch. Jack says it is like watching a show on television where the film has been time exposed. The primroses literally burst into shimmering luminous yellow blooms which stay until sunrise. When the sun touches them in the early morning, they wilt away and die, those startlingly beautiful blossoms gone forever.

Margaret Ware has several chairs out beside the primrose bed because once you start watching, you are too mesmerized to leave for quite a while. Children love to race from flower to flower, calling out in absolute glee when they see one about to "pop." They never want to leave when it is time to go home, begging to wait for "just one more."

If you are a close friend to Margaret Ware, she is apt to give you a pair of scissors to clip off the wilted flowers from the night before as you sit watching the new ones arrive. It is hard for her to keep up with the trimming during the "high season" of the July primroses. These plants reseed themselves and sometimes Margaret Ware worries because the crop is a lot more scarce than the year before. But, seemingly for no reason at all, the following year the flowers will be abundant. There is no necessity to call before you go, because every evening you will find several of the locals out around the bed when the time is ripe. And there is always an extra pair of scissors.

Weisenberger Mill

One of the most beautiful afternoon drives in the Bluegrass begins at Midway, goes south to the Old Frankfort Pike, east to Payne's Depot Road, north to the Weisenberger Mill Road, and west back to Midway. You pass multiple historic sites along this route, including one of the oldest and most memorable, the Weisenberger Mill. This operation, the oldest flour mill in Kentucky that is still in use, lies just to the north of picturesque Elkhorn Creek in Scott County, but its address and its heart have always belonged to Midway. To appreciate the legacy that it brings to the area, you would need to know a capsule of the history of this mill and its owners.

Augustus Weisenberger, born in Baden, Germany in 1820, was the first of that family to set foot in Woodford County. He came to Spring Station as a machinist for the Alexander family, and ended up building a small buhrstone mill there at the big spring, which he operated until 1870. He then purchased a three-story stone mill on Elkhorn Creek that had been built by Robert Rusk* who had built the dam at this location in 1818. One of the most important innovations Augustus adopted after his purchase was to convert to the roller process in 1887 which increased his production

Robert Rusk is sometimes listed as Robert Risk

61

from thirty-five barrels a day to fifty. Augustus died in 1902 and his business was turned over to his son Philip.

Philip was born at Spring Station in 1868, and soon after birth he was introduced to milling. When he took over the mill in 1902, Philip decided to take down the old stone structure, grind it into the concrete and use this material to erect a new building. In 1913 this new mill was state of the art in every way. The twenty-thousand-bushel, iron-clad elevator built in 1904 enabled him to produce seventy-five barrels a day. Philip bought all his grain from local farmers, putting approximately one hundred thousand dollars back into his community's economy yearly. At the time, the mill was known as "Weisenberger's Sanitary Flour Mill" and it produced "Ten Broeck Flour" and "Purity Water Ground Meal." The Weisenbergers distributed their wares to stores in horse drawn wagons.

Philip's son Augustus (Gus) came into the business in 1918 and sold flour, meal, and feed to merchants in all the surrounding areas. When Gus' son, fourth generation Phil, went to work for the mill, they were renting a warehouse in Lexington to keep their stock there, ready to be delivered. They had nearly all the business around central Kentucky, using about twenty workers and five trucks. Because of rising expenses this procedure became incredibly costly to operate even though they had the lion's share of the market in the area.

Thus, when Gus died in 1955, Phil decided to make a change and go into mixes and food service rather than to raise prices to make a profit. It took him from 1955 until 1975 to complete this change. He began by making chicken batter for Jerry's Restaurants and then made the glaze for their strawberry pie. He first packaged the pancake and biscuit mixes. Now the list has been expanded to include all kinds of flour, cornmeal, grits, bran, fish batter, and mixes for hot rolls, pizza crusts, raspberry muffins, cornbread, hushpuppies, spoonbread, funnel cakes, and others.

Phil's son Mac has now become the proud owner of the business, and his son Philip works for his dad. Philip is the sixth generation of Weisenbergers who have devoted their time and energy towards making this family establishment a source of pride and distinction. There has always been the threat of flooding because the mill is located right on the brink of the waters of the south Elkhorn. These floods were usually not devastating to the Weisenbergers because benchmarks could be watched and when they would get to a certain point, all the milling and office paraphernalia would be moved to another building for safe keeping. However, there was one horrendous exception, on the first of March in 1997. Phil states, "When we left the mill on Saturday night, we all felt it was going to be OK. On Sunday I got up real early. Mac had already been out there, and he saw my car at the Midway grocery. He said, 'We're finished, Dad.'"

They went together out to the mill and looked with horror at the damage from the raging Elkhorn. Phil admits, "There's no way on earth I can describe the feeling we had when we saw the destruction." But the family pulled together, friends came to help, and the long road to restoration was begun. Mac was put in charge of the cleanup; more than forty-nine motors were removed and sent out to bake out and dry; Phil's other son Jay worked to dry out and restore the computer back up data; Phil reprinted all the sales orders which had been washed away; and with the help of co-packers, they were able to notify customers that their orders would be ready in a week. And miraculously, they were. It was an amazing feat of will power and endurance.

In Kerr's History of Kentucky, old Augustus was described as "a man of fidelity and honesty, who is held in high esteem by his associates and who proved worthy in his citizenship and faithful in his friendships." In the same book, Philip J. was declared to be "known for his industry and integrity." As you drive past the wonderful old landmark on Elkhorn Creek today, you can rest assured that the same durable qualities that were so ardently admired in the family generations ago can be found in abundance in the inhabitants of the modern day Weisenberger Mill.

Autumn

"I watched "Our Town" by Thornton Wilder on PBS last night and it was incredible. I cried at the end when Emily says, "Oh, earth, you're too wonderful for anybody to realize you. Do any human beings ever realize life while they live it? – every, every minute?" And the Stage Manager answers, "No." This play has always reminded me so much of Midway."

Personal Journal
October, 1984

Biker's Brunch

There was a special ritual of fall for a number of years in the 1980s. The participants of this pilgrimage, forty-five Woodford Countians and their friends, were all ages, male and female, and ranged from being professionals to students and all levels in between. Someone would choose one Saturday in November and send out cards to all interested parties. Then Shakertown at Pleasant Hill would have to be phoned in order to reserve the entire Tanyard House for the night of the expedition. The last duty of the organizer would be to notify Mary Ann McCauley.

This annual bicycle ride from Versailles to Shakertown, a distance of about twenty miles down Highway 33, would not have been so difficult if it hadn't been for the formidable hill that extends for a couple of miles on the far side of the Kentucky River, along the Palisades. As it was, the ride was an endurance test for even the youngest and most robust, and it would have been next to impossible without the hospitality of the McCauleys.

The bikers would meet at a corner in downtown Versailles with their wheels of all description. One couple finally resorted to motorbikes, but most would come on ten speeds, five speeds, and a few on the old flat handle-barred bikes with fat tires. Some would appear in fashionable ensembles, but most in blue jeans and Nikes.

They would be carrying water or Gatorade and a good bit of courage. At the appointed time the trek would start out Main Street in the midst of great hullabaloos and clamor, followed by a pickup truck (SAG Wagon) to rescue any and all saggers who for whatever reason would have to give up the adventure. This truck was driven by Ben Chandler whose wife Toss was one of the bikers every year.

The best part of the trip, which would make the entire effort infinitely worthwhile, was Mary Ann McCauley's Brunch for the Bikers. Mary Ann and her husband Graham own a beautiful piece of property off Troy Pike named Trojan Farm. In the 1970s they meticulously restored an old two-story log house on this farm that had been in Graham's family since before the Civil War. They added enough space to the original house to make it one of the County's most beautiful – as well as most comfortable – houses. Located just about half-way from Versailles to Shakertown, it would have made a perfect stop for the bikers just to rest a few minutes, to repair their bikes and bodies, and then go on with their journey.

But Mary Ann would not hear of this. Each year she prepared a marvelous brunch that simply saved the day for most of the cyclists. Very early in the mornings on the day of the rides, she would carry her handmade road signs of encouragement towards Versailles and place them in the manor of the old Burma Shave ads. Like Burma Shave, there would be four signs to a unit, placed several feet apart and the lines would rhyme. She thought they would cheer on the bikers who were beginning to sag;

Hooray for the cyclist

You've come so far.

Now is your last chance

To go by car!

Peddle fast

Or peddle slow

You've still a lot

More hills to go.

If that last hill

Got you down

Just remember you're only

Halfway from town!

Forget the ache

Forget the pain

Just keep on peddling

Are you sure you're sane?

BIKER'S BRUNCH

Her menus were unbelievable. In 1986 she served:

Water

Coffee with Brandy

Bloody Marys

Juice

Chicken Livers wrapped in bacon

(one hundred and forty of these)

Sausage and egg casserole

Homemade bread

Old country ham on homemade biscuits

Assorted fruit plate

Melody of cookies

Sock-it-to-me coffee cake

In other years she served such wonderful delicacies as spinach quiche, hot spiced tomato broth, marinated raw broccoli, stuffed dates and crab meat dip. These were ultimate brunches that the bikers would never forget. Mary Ann would also invite neighbors and friends who were not riding to cheer the bikers as they crossed the cattle gate into Trojan Farm. That was pretty heady stuff for the ones who were about to pass out. The encouragement and the pause – but mostly the food – carried the cyclists on through the rest of their exhausting day.

The bad part of the ride would come within striking distance of the Shakertown Village. This was the climb of the hill on the far side of the Kentucky River, where the road goes up a steep incline for a couple of miles, with no flat surface where you could relax and lightly peddle for a few minutes to catch your breath. It was a test of anybody's mettle to even try this stretch, and some bikers would have to get off and push for a few minutes to keep going.

Once on top of this hill, the rest would be easy, and you could almost coast into the village and down to the Tanyard House. The bikers would roll off their bikes onto the lawn to catch their breath and to revel in the knowledge that they had completed the difficult ride once again. With the help of Mary Ann, they finished the pilgrimage without the SAG Wagon. The young people would be laughing and talking and planning things to do in Shakertown, still full of energy. But the older ones would be lying on their backs in the grass looking up in the beautiful blue sky, gasping for air, and utterly exhausted, but feeling proud. That night the group of all ages would sit around a fire in the fireplace in the old Tanyard House and tell ghost stories. In that setting these stories struck and added fear in the faint-hearted as they listened until the wee small hours in the morning. Lynn Kelley loved this part of the adventure so much that he rarely went to sleep at all.

Thanksgiving Market

The Christian Church in Midway, organized in July of 1844 and the second oldest church in the town, has always been very active in community affairs. Their project anticipated the most for years and years by the locals was the Thanksgiving Market, which was sponsored by the Christian Women's Fellowship of the church, and attended by more people than anyone could count by the time it had to be abandoned in the 1990s. At the time of its demise, it had been held for over seventy years and had just become too popular with too many people coming to browse the bazaar and to eat the marvelous luncheon.

It all started with the parishioners who lived in the country and the parish townspeople exchanging items on the day before Thanksgiving. Money from the exchanges went to the church. Soon the ladies decided to go together and make lunch to eat that day. The menu they chose was chicken salad and oyster stew which they would all join together to make in the church kitchen, and the ladies would bring home-baked pies to the feast. It wasn't long until friends and relatives heard about this delicious lunch being served at the church, and they wanted to come. The church ladies were making beautiful crafts to sell to each other as well, and this news traveled fast.

One problem that they soon faced was lack of space, because people from all over Central Kentucky began to mark that day on the calendar as a time to spend shopping in Midway and eating lunch before heading home. The market quickly outgrew the small basement room in the church and was moved to the old kitchen on top of the sanctuary. This area required going up and down many steps, not a good solution. Finally, they were able to use a large room that had been erected next to the church building, and this took care of the ever increasing number for the luncheon for several years.

The fate of the Market was also sealed by the great percentage of the young women of the church deciding to go to work. This cut down on the number of people free to cut up all the chicken, pecans and celery to say nothing of waiting on tables. (By this time, the amounts of the ingredients had doubled and redoubled to eighty-two hens, four-quart jars of chopped celery, and eight pounds of pecans. Not to be done in an hour's time.)

Lily Walden, who was making the delicious oyster stew from a family recipe, was using thirteen gallons of fresh oysters, seven quarts of half and half, twelve gallons of whole milk, and six quarts of whipping cream. When Lily was no longer up to the huge responsibility of making the stew to perfection, she entrusted her two daughters-in-law with the recipe, and they carried on the tradition as long as the church had the Market.

To save the Market, the men in the church were called upon to help, and the date was moved back a week to give the exhausted church members time to recuperate before their own family's Thanksgiving feasts. Friends from the other churches volunteered to help because NO ONE wanted the Market to end. But when it could no longer be carried out in a style fitting for the CWF, the wonderful event was forced to close

To get ready for what would turn out to be the final Market day, a few friends from other churches had gathered with CWF faithful workers to cut up the chicken. When the pastor came into the room, he spotted one friend who was Catholic, cutting up chicken to beat the band. He jokingly asked her if she had genuflected when she came in. "No," she answered. "But I will when I leave." The exchange brought about a good laugh.

Midway will always miss the Thanksgiving Market which marked the beginning of the Holiday season. It was a day of rejoicing together with friends and neighbors, the like of which will probably not be seen again.

Smoke Gets in Your Eyes

The sense of smell is by far the strongest sense that mankind possesses. You can see a person that you knew in high school but cannot remember his name. You can hear a piece of music but cannot recall the title or who wrote it or where you heard it last. You can taste a tangy drink but cannot for the life of you remember just what it is or when you tasted it before. But an aroma lasts forever. If you catch a whiff of a shaving lotion that a boy you once knew wore when you went with him to a Sunday afternoon movie back in 1950, you are immediately transported back to the neighborhood theatre with that young man and his wonderful aftershave. You will forever connect that scent with that young man. So, it is with the burning of leaves.

No one burns leaves anymore because it's not allowed. "They say" it creates pollution and could cause accidents for drivers of cars that happen to come by your house when the leaves are smoking. And "they say" the fires are dangerous no matter how careful you are. But if you are driving down a country lane in your car in the fall and happen upon a farmer burning a few fence posts in the meadow, the smell permeates the air and you remember the joy of raking leaves and burning them in the fall.

SMOKE GETS IN YOUR EYES

The children would be hanging around waiting for you to get a fairly large pile raked up so they could take a running leap in the air and come down in the middle of them. Over and over. You would finally get the leaves to the edge of your lawn at your street in a tall straight line and light the end ones with a match. Dry and crisp, they would ignite immediately. As they burned down the line, you had to be close by with your rake gathering the newly fallen few into the fire, stirring up the ashes. The raking and burning would take at least five hours of the day. It was such a delightfully simple way to rid yourself of leaves.

When the fire was completely out and the ashes cooled, you would leave the outdoors and go into the house. Your clothes, hands, hair, and shoes would smell of burning leaves, and there is nothing in the world that closely resembles it. You would be reluctant to take your bath and wash your hair, knowing that this would take away the last aroma of Autumn and force you to accept the passing of yet another season.

WARREN MITCHELL

Our Group

There is a group of men who meet downtown Midway three mornings a week to drink coffee together and socialize. This group has been meeting for over thirty years at various places and at different times, but these men have always found the time and the place to come together. Their topics of conversation usually center around farming, the weather, the community, and politics, but there are wonderfully humorous old stories that they love to tell and hear time and time again. Some of the original members have died, of course, and some do not come frequently, but there are a few who wouldn't miss it for the world. In the summer of the year 2000, the group was meeting at the Eagles Trading Post Restaurant. Guwynn Campbell, Rex Cecil, Les Duncan, Brereton Jones (former Governor of Kentucky), Bill Clark, and nonagenarian Warren Mitchell were present at their July 22nd gathering.

Mr. Mitchell: "I think a lot about mules because we worked with them. They were good animals. But this story is about an old man who knew he wasn't going to live too long. He had three sons. He was a big farmer, and he wrote his will. He divided what he had to his three sons, but he didn't just divide it in three ways, he willed to them what they needed most. He knew what they were all short on, what they needed. So, everything worked out fine til he got to the mules. They got the mules brought up into the lot and counted them, and they had seventeen. Well, the old man had said he wanted one of the sons to have half of the mules, one a third, and one a ninth. That's when they counted them and they had seventeen. They said, 'Well, we can't do that.' About then they saw their old friend, Mr. Brown, riding his mule down the road. They said, 'Hello, Mr. Brown. Come and see us.' He went on up and put his reins down and he counted the mules. He said, 'Well one of you can have half and one a third and one a ninth, and you got seventeen mules in there. And he puts his mule in, and that made eighteen. 'Now,' he says, 'We're in business. You get half of them,' and he put out nine. 'Now,' he said, 'you get a third,' and he put out six, 'Six and nine are fifteen and that works fine. And the fellow that gets a ninth gets two. Fifteen and two is seventeen.' Mr. Brown got on his mule and rode on down the road."

Brereton Jones: "You know, one of the most fun times I had with this group was after the election and Sue Wiley and several of the reporters were around the capital and were talking to me about things. And I said, 'What you need to do is come over to see the brain trust of this administration.' I said, 'The people that are going to be making the decisions on most things meet on every Saturday morning in Midway.' They looked at me and said, 'Is that right?' I said, 'That's absolutely right. You need to come over and talk to them.' And so she came over. Remember when Sue came over? And brought a couple of tv people who brought cameras and they interviewed, and Warren told them the mule story, and after that whenever I got a question that was maybe a little difficult to answer, I'd say, 'I'm going to have to confer with my group in Midway before I give you an answer on that one.'"

Guwynn Campbell: "Ken Speers came for a couple of years to our meetings after the sewing factory closed, but he hasn't been here for maybe a year. When Logan owned that store down the street, one day Sweets Riddle* pulled his truck up to that restaurant. Ken made the trick up with Logan. They went in the store and loaded Sweets Riddles' truck down with clothes right off the rack. Then when Sweets came out, they were going to get the police to arrest him for stealing clothes from Logan's."

*Sweets Riddle, another of "Our Group" for years, is deceased.

Les Duncan joined in: "One time they were shooting a commercial over there for Logan, and Ken Speers walked in there, and the people had everything set up. He started moving people around. Says, 'You get right over there, you get over here.' The producer, WLEX, I believe it was, came around and asked Logan, 'Who is that guy?' Logan says, 'He's my executive producer.' Ken moved them all around and walked out."

Mr. Mitchell added another story: "Well there were two guys, and one of them had a lot of respect about what he knew about racehorses. One of them bought a horse and the other one thought, 'Well, durn, that must be a right good horse if he bought him.' And then the first guy said, 'I guess I made a mistake cause that guy is a good horseman and he wanted that horse.' So, he bought him back and paid a little extra. And they did this about five times. A stranger heard about it and he said 'That must be a mighty good horse. I think I'll slip in there and buy him.' And he did. Then the first man went back to buy the horse again and the second man said, 'Oh, I sold him to the old Mr. John.' 'Oh, Hell!' he said, 'Why'd you do that? We's making plenty of money out of that horse.'"

After several more stories, Guwynn Campbell, and Les Duncan talked about the beginning of the group meetings. They said that the first men that met were "Warren and Sweets and Yeary." (To which Mr. Mitchell laconically declared that "The sad part of it is that they are all dead except me. I'm bound to be next.") The first time, they just went in to get a sandwich; then they started meeting regularly. They called themselves "Our Group." The first place they met was the Midway Café, then Woolum's, and they declared that every place they chose went out of business. The other day Mr. Cambell laughingly asked the lady in charge of the restaurant where they meet now that if she gets ready to run them out, let them know ahead of time so they can find another place.

They meet for just an hour each time, and when they leave, they put up a dollar or two each for the waitress who brings the coffee. Mr. Campbell summed the mornings up nicely, "Now that's all we've talked about for years. You just come in here and laugh about silly things. It does you more good than the doctor's medicine. I tell you. And if you don't get to come or you miss it, why the day seems twice as long."

'Big Bad John'

Jim Bowling, my brother-in-law, was involved with country music for as long as I can remember. He was in charge of the first Philip Morris Country Music shows that are given just before the Kentucky Derby every year. Although he knew and admired Johnny Cash, Patsy Cline, and several other "stars," his best country music friend was Jimmy Dean. He and Jimmy ended up owning some racehorses together. One fall day several years ago, Jim phoned us with the news that he and Jimmy were coming to look at some horses at Three Chimneys Farm in Woodford County, and that they just might be able to spend the night with us, if it wasn't too much trouble. Of course, we were excited to death, and I said it would be no trouble at all.

Then I went upstairs to look at the rooms where they would be staying, and it was a different story. The only presentable room for guests was Jenny's old room, but its bathroom would have to be shared with our two children who were still at home. This meant that bedroom would have to be my brother-in-law's, and I felt sheer panic over what would be Jimmy's. The only solution was that he would have to be in our own bedroom, as it had the sole private bath in the house. But our room was a disaster. I pulled the curtains out and saw that the backs were worn from sunlight to a degree that it could not be hidden. The sheets and towels were so old that they looked grey. There was no decent cover for the bed. I was aghast.

We had two children in college and two more that were going, so we had not spent unnecessary money on the house during those years. My mind raced uncontrollable for a couple of hours. Then I made my list.

First, I went to Lexington and bought one entire set of really good bath towels (they were Ralph Lauren's, cream colored,) one set of linen sheets and pillowcases, one mattress cover, a set of deep-piled hand towels, and a huge woolen blanket to go on the bed, along with a new coverlet. Everything would be new except the carpet. I also picked up every cassette I could find of Jimmy's music that we didn't already own so we would be familiar with ALL of it.

The next day Jack and I took down our curtains and put them in the trash. We went into our other daughter's room and removed her wooden slatted Venetian blinds and installed them in our bedroom. We went through all the other bedrooms and switched paintings and prints from all over the upstairs into our room to make it look more interesting. We hung anything we could find on the nails emptied by this exercise, thinking Jimmy would not see these other rooms. We moved clothes out of our closet to make room for his things. We were exhausted, but finally we were ready.

Jim called on the day they might arrive. Their schedule had become too complicated, and they would not be able to spend the night with us. He was truly sorry. They might have time to come by, but he really doubted it. That afternoon around four, after I had given up, they appeared at my BACK door. They walked through my totally disheveled kitchen to the den. I was delighted to see Jim and thrilled to meet Jimmy. He was great. He liked the house and bragged on our daughters' pictures. He sat down at our hideously out-of-tune piano and played an old Irving Berlin song and sang it. At my request, he seemed pleased to do his famous "Big Bad John" in that incredible voice.

He said he needed something for his sore throat, so we went up to the doctor's office. We slipped into the emergency room just inside the back door so he wouldn't be seen by the patients. But soon all the office girls lined up in the hallway to meet him and to get autographs. In checking him over, Jack looked in his ears, and, trying to make conversation, asked him if he had been out to Three Chimneys Farm. Jimmy said, "No. Why'd you ask? Do you see horse manure in my ear?" He is a funny man, gracious and nice. After they left for Louisville, we decided to name the new beautiful wool blanket "The Big Bad John" in memory of his visit.

ANN FISHER

Spare Us

Three out of our four children chose to swim competitively in grade school and high school. This was a real commitment as the closest available swim team practiced in Lexington every day for ten months of the year, a trip of at least twenty minutes up and twenty minutes home for us. Once involved in such a project, it becomes a natural thing to do with your day. Casseroles cooked in a time-baked oven at nine o-clock at night take on a tastier quality than you had imagined possible when you were young. The friendships between both the parents and the children on the team became as close as family. The exercise and discipline were so good for the children mentally and physically that we all felt the time spent was unquestionably worthwhile.

One bonus for us was that we could drive back and forth to practice on the beautiful Old Frankfort Pike, which is lovely any time of day, any time of year. But our favorite times became sunrise and sunset in the winter. There was one long stretch of time when the drive was even more interesting to me and my swimmers – seven-year-old daughter Ann, and her ten-year-old brother, Peter.

One of the most beautiful farms along the way had been sold to a very wealthy man and he decided to put in ponds, ridges, bridges, and several incredible barns where none had existed before. During this construction, the children delighted in watching the changes becoming evident before their eyes.

But the downside was that a lot of the topsoil from the farm would go washing down the pike in times of rain. Now, topsoil in the Bluegrass region is not like soil in any other area in the country. My brother-in-law used to tell how he wanted to take a quart jar of it back home with him to sell by the teaspoon on the corners of Manhattan. He vowed it would sell like hotcakes. So it bothered me a lot to watch this rich, brown earth being washed randomly down along the side of the road. And I guess I never failed to lecture the children about how I felt.

One Saturday morning just at daylight the three of us were making our way up the Old Frankfort Pike in the rain to the GLSA swimming pool in Lexington. I noticed that Peter had fallen asleep in the back seat, as he often did when practice was that early in the day. Annie was in the front passenger seat with her head tilted back against the headrest with her eyes closed, and I assumed that she was asleep as well. As we approached the farm, the soil was gushing down the sides of the road, and I must have let out a great mournful sigh. Without opening her eyes or moving her head from its position on the seat, Annie said in a low, tired voice, "SPARE us the talk about the topsoil."

The Big Apple

One of the most rewarding family excursions in Woodford County is a sojourn out to Garrett's Orchard on Shannon Run Road. As you turn onto the narrow graveled farm lane that leads to the big grey barn on the hill, you ride past row upon row of raspberry and blackberry bushes that are loaded down with fruit in the summer for you to "pick your own." The barn serves as a market where fresh produce, frozen apple slush, delicious jams, jellies, relishes, and many other items may be bought all year. In the fall the main attraction is apples – all kinds of varieties – and the orchard where you may pick your own is located on the far side of the barn. There are baskets of apples inside all ready for you to buy if you want, but the fun is in the picking. To take your family out on a chilly fall day to choose their own apples and put them in a basket to take home is a delight that they will remember the rest of their lives.

In 1948, Joe Garrett was the proud owner of the orchard, and the market was located just down the road at Highland Place. Here James Watkins and his sons had built a shed where the produce was displayed and apple cider was chilled just right for on-the-spot drinking. Mr. Watkins was a man from Breathitt County who had four boys and they all worked at the orchard for several years.

The old shed had a wonderful system for dividing apples by size. The apples would be put on a contraption that was like a big open weave chain. It was about twenty-four inches wide, and its woven squares were a different size so the small fruit would drop first as the big chain moved, then the midsized, and so on to the largest. Back then, apples were sold by size. Now they are sold by weight and the large orchards have electronic devices that even sort by color. Watching the apples move up the big chain and drop was one of the main attractions of the orchard for the children.

Joe was the first in Kentucky to use the method of "you pick" for berries. He fell into using it out of sheer desperation. He had been paying pocket change to some grade schoolers to pick for him. One day he found out they were lining the bottom of the quart containers with leaves or rocks, just having a good time. He was so angry with them that he sent them packing on the spot and told them they would have to come back the next day to collect any money owed them. There were several customers there waiting for the berries, and he told them if they really wanted the fruit they would have to go and pick for themselves. He handed them the quart containers, and a new custom had been born for Garrett's Orchard.

Joe then became interested in the dwarf apple tree because the customer would also be able to pick from these for himself. With the taller tree you couldn't allow people to climb up to get to the fruit because of liability. Even without the "you-pick" problem, it was imperative to take a look at the dwarf trees because labor was getting hard to find for that kind of work. There was also the efficiency factor of producing fruit on a smaller frame. In his grandfather's day it would take twenty leaves to produce an apple while the dwarf tree could do it with ten.

Joe raised peach trees for a few years, but was forced to stop as the crop was not dependable. The sad probability is that in this area you might get three good crops in ten years, However, he considers the peach a "wonderful queen of fruits." He says you have to be really close up on the picking. For the best flavor, you should pick them when they're almost soft, not firm. But if you're going to haul them even a hundred miles, you have to pick them "hard ripe." So, if you are planning on peaches as a money crop, the temptation is to pick them for color rather than for ripeness and the flavor is not the same.

Garrett's Orchard is a wonderful part of Woodford County history. William Garrett came to Kentucky in 1774 in the company of John Harrod and settled on one thousand acres of land in Woodford County that he was able to claim. His great-grandson, Joseph Garrett (born in 1866) had a great love of saddle horses, and he was one of the owners of the famous Black Squirrel. In the decade of the 1890s, there was a terrible crash in the horse business and Joseph began to look for an alternative way to make a living.

He had always been interested in growing fruit. He began an orchard in 1895 that contained fifty acres. Then he heard of John Kaenzig, who was living in a Swiss colony over at East Bernstadt, Kentucky. He heard that Mr. Kaenzig had come over from Switzerland and had brought Swiss horticultural knowledge with him. Joseph decided to go see him and to try to persuade Mr. Kaenzig to come to help plant his orchard. He was successful in his quest, and they began planting fruit trees in Woodford County. Sadly, Joseph died in his forties and his son was more interested in cattle and tobacco than he was in raising fruit trees. It was Joseph's grandson Joe who put on the mantle of his grandfather's dream and expanded the orchard operation.

Garrett's Orchard is an institution that the entire community can be proud of. The parking lot of the big grey barn is usually filled with the cars of people from the city and countryside who want to feel the pride that comes with choosing and picking their own apples and berries. The new ones have wisely kept the name of "Garrett's Orchard" because of the deserved reputation that it has been able to maintain since 1897.

To Market, To Market

During the past fifty years, stores have come and gone in Midway with regularity. The town has lost Logan's, the Midway Drug Store, the hardware store, a few dress shops, a barbershop, the Red Brick house, and several grocery stores to name a few. But one market that has remarkable staying power is the grocery that is located inside the "V" where US 62 breaks away from Winter Street down by the entrance of Parrish Hill Farm. This store has gone by different names and has had several owners, but it has endured the test of time. And it has kept its wonderful character.

To step inside is an experience. The floor slants towards the back of the store. The shelves are very close together and are always overloaded with stock. The aisles are just wide enough for one basket to roll down at a time – there is no passing place except at the narrow ends. During watermelon season when the melons are placed on the floor at the base of one shelf, even a single basket may not be able to weave through without special maneuvering. Midway has been blessed to have this market like no other.

Three owners of this grocery store had a lot in common. They uniformly treated people right, were kind, helpful, accommodating, and ordered what the customers wanted. They kept the shelves full and tried their best to keep the produce fresh, which is hard to do sometimes because little markets tend to get what's left over on the truck. But the owners have consistently offered service with a smile and have done the very best they could.

Roberta and Elwood House owned the grocery in the early 1950s. Midway still had a high school, and when the ball team would come home from an away game, they would stop at the store, along with the cheerleaders. There would be cokes and hamburgers for all, pay as you could. It was the place for the teenagers to unwind and have some fun before going home.

Roberta remembers one winter when the snow was so deep that delivery trucks could not get through, and the store ran out of bread. Elwood thought about the train that came regularly from Lexington, so he called the Honey Krust Bread Company up there and asked them to send down as much as they could spare on the afternoon train. Mr. Tom Roach brought a pickup truck and he and Elwood met the train. They filled the truck full to overflowing and took it to the store. When the townspeople learned that the market had fresh bread there was a great crush of folks waiting in line in a very few minutes. Many customers had to come on foot through the snow, but that was a small price to pay.

A second owner, Ida Lee Craig, tells about the time when she decided to stay up very late to get the store cleaned up for the next day's business. She and her husband, Marshall, lived upstairs over the grocery, and that night he went on to bed to rest up from the busy day. Around two in the morning, Ida Lee was mopping up the last aisle of the store when she heard a distinct knocking at the door. She cautiously peered through the glass and recognized a valued customer. She opened up the door, sure of an emergency. The customer put on her best smile and said, "I saw your light on as I was driving by, and I just knew you wouldn't mind letting me have a pack of cigarettes." Ida Lee laughingly obliged.

Chuck Bradley, another beloved owner of the store, and his family arrived from California in 1979, coming "home" to look after aging family members. He had never been in the grocery business before, but he decided that was something he would like to do. At that opportune time, the Midway Market just happened to be put up for sale, the dream of the Bradley family.

Chuck lengthened the store hours from six o'clock in the morning to ten at night. He started opening on Sundays, a convenience not extended before. Gasoline tanks were installed to make the little grocery a full-service station. It became a popular place to stand around, drink coffee and socialize almost any time of day.

In one of Chuck's favorite tales about the market, one early morning two young men filled their gasoline tank up and drove off without paying. Chuck has an absolute line which you wouldn't want to cross, and these youths had crossed it. There followed a wild chase on the Old Frankfort Pike, then back through Midway to the interstate after they made an attempt to run him off the road, and a race up the I-64 at ninety mph. Chuck finally caught up with them in Lexington at a red light with a police car nearby. Thinking about it later, he said, "I learned something. You just don't chase. It's not worth it."

The Midway Market is the kind of place that defines this town. Long may it continue.

Winter

"I love winter. I even enjoy the hardships of winter, when people need other people to get along. I love the winter nights of tv and games with the children, the fire in the fireplace, and the popcorn. Even of having to walk to the grocery in minus five weather. When you take deep breaths, you can feel the air go down to your stomach. Winter makes you re-evaluate your life and helps you to realize what is important."

Personal Journal
February, 1984

Winter Snow

It doesn't snow in Kentucky now as much as it has in earlier years. At least it doesn't seem to snow as much. There were times in Midway when the roads would be closed off because of drifts, and the town would have to go without fresh milk, bread and other dairy products until the snowplows could get through. Even the mail was not delivered. Sometimes it would be three to four days. Of course, the county snow removal equipment wasn't as plentiful or proficient, and that made a lot of difference. Some days an announcer on the radio would state that only emergency vehicles would be allowed to use the road, and the only road that would be open to them would be the interstate. The state patrolman would be checking the exits. The Midway-Versailles Pike is always dangerous in the snow because the winds seem to crisscross it west to east, causing drifts that could end up six feet deep.

For the people whose jobs and well-being meant they had to get out, the days of bad weather were a nightmare. But for the ones who could stay home and enjoy it, these days were golden. Especially for the children because the big snows meant no school until ALL the country roads were clear, and this afforded a winter holiday that wasn't anticipated.

Hats, mittens, scarves, snowsuits and boots were brought out of storage, sized up and crammed on. The lucky children that would still fit into last year's wear would be calling their friends to come on out by nine o'clock, and by lunch time, snowmen, forts, and igloos would be sprouting up all over the neighborhood. There would be snowball fights and angel-wings and snow-cream and tunnels. Older ambitious children would be coming by all morning, asking if they could shovel walks even while the snow was still falling. Cars would be stuck about five feet out of the garages, looking for all the world like they belonged there as part of the landscape. Neighbor would assist neighbor at getting the cars out, and often children would run around behind the pushers, having the time of their lives, throwing snowballs at the car, the pushers and at each other. The world looks even more gorgeous under a blanket of freshly fallen snow, and people would be out with cameras to get a "shot" before there were any tracks or melting. Phone calls were made to the elderly and to shut-ins, reassuring them that they would be looked after, and that someone would get to them if they needed groceries or medicine. People who had a fireplace carried in loads of wood in the afternoon to be burned that night when the family was all together, playing board games that hadn't been out of the closet since last winter. There was a wonderful feeling of hunkering down and getting through the crunch together.

For the children, it was pure joy. Just at the northern edge of Midway is Parrish Hill Farm. The house sits on the crest of a huge steep hill that slopes down to Lee's Branch, which runs its course across the farm towards South Elkhorn Creek. Sledding never got any better than careening down that hill towards the branch, with children – and very often grown-ups – screaming with joy and a little bit of fear that the old sled might get such a good run that it wouldn't stop until it went into the water. Old and new sleds with runners were used, as well as the newly discovered saucers that the younger children liked so much. And one year some teenage boys went down the hill all season on the upside-down hood of an old car they had dismantled. The older children took turns with the younger ones, often helping them up after a spill, and were careful not to run into them on the slope.

The Roach family, owners of Parrish Hill, delighted in the fact that their hill was the most popular spot in town when it snowed, and they usually built a huge fire at the top of the hill where the sledders could warm themselves between flights. Sometimes there would be hot dogs and marshmallows to roast to add to the festivities, and there would always be hot chocolate and cookies in the big old house before everyone went home. Finally, the sledders would reluctantly call it a day. But not before they made their plans for the next morning – to meet at Parrish Hill.

Skating at Stonewall

Stonewall Farm, one of the most beautiful and historical farms in Woodford County, lies about halfway between Midway and Versailles on the pike that connects the two towns. It has a magnificent stone wall that borders the entire frontage of the property. Major Warren Viley, the owner of the farm, commissioned John Kearney, an Irishman, to build the wall in 1863. It is known for sure who built it and when it was completed because the wall is signed and dated, and it is one of the only two such documented walls still standing in Kentucky. This magnificent structure has required no maintenance for over one hundred and thirty years, except for the places knocked down by vehicles that have crashed into it. Mr. Kearney's wall, built to last, has a foundation two feet underground and is thirty-six inches wide at the base. The stones gently slope up to measure eighteen inches across the top. It is a dry wall, built without mortar.

A funny story about Mr. Kearney was reported in *The Woodford Sun* many years ago. When he was well into the task of building his wall, a gentleman from Versailles came riding along the pike in his buggy and he stopped to watch the master artist at work. The man said, "Tell me, my man, just how much is Mr. Viley paying you by the yard to build that wall?"

Mr. Kearney looked up from his labor and asked in his Irish brogue, "Can you kape a sakrat?"

"Indeed I can," the man assured him.

"Well, sir, so can I," replied Mr. Kearney, and leaned back into his work.

Stonewall Farm was the renowned thoroughbred nursery of Major Viley, who gave the mare Black Bess to General John Hunt Morgan, his mount during the Civil War. The mare saved the general's life on his memorable ride from Lebanon to Carthage.

Stonewall was the site of many historic barbecues given by Major Viley as political rallies for his friends, including John C. Breckinridge, J.C.S. Blackburn, James B. Beck and Senator Henry L. Martin. Given in the woodland adjacent to the homeplace, these were attended by hundreds of people who were eager to partake of the Major's hospitality.

But the moon and the stars never shone brighter on Stonewall than on a magical evening in the 1960s when friends gathered there to roast marshmallows and hot dogs beside a blazing fire. They had come together to ice skate on an enormous pond that had sprung from the ground as a result of overflowing the Big Sink, a phenomenon that rises every now and again. The Big Sink water covers large surfaces of land and then disappears underground to passages that allow it to flow through after it soaks down by way of sink holes. On this night in the 1960s, the Big Sink water had covered about two acres of Stonewall with two and a half feet of water and then had frozen over. Incredibly, the surface was smooth.

The farm belonged to the Starks family at this time, and Dick and Hilda decided that this was an opportunity not to be missed. On a Monday afternoon, they called sixty-five people to come out for the evening to ice skate and sixty-one showed up. Very few had skates, but no one wanted to miss the night. Dick built a huge fire to keep the non-skaters warm and for roasting hot dogs and marshmallows. The moon was full and made it easy to see the skaters flowing back and forth between the trees that were rising through the ice, standing like Longfellow's "Druids of eld."* Whether it was the rarity of the Big Sink water freezing smooth – or the moonlight – or the camaraderie of the friends – there was a magic in the air that night that would not be felt again in a lifetime.

* Evangeline

Old Friends Revisited

Winter is the only time you have to devote entire afternoons to reading anymore. Nothing is more pleasurable than to take a big book to the den after lunch, poke up the fire in the fireplace, and stretch out on the couch to read. The dishes have been done, the laundry was done yesterday, and bills do not have to be paid until tomorrow. If it were spring, summer or fall, there would be yard work staring at you, because yard work is everlasting. But in winter, sometimes you can manage to catch your breath and take an hour or two for leisure.

It is important on these afternoons that you have something on the shelf that you are anxious to read. Otherwise, you will spend your time wandering around the house, looking desperately for something that will entertain you. Keep something in stock that you've purchased in the fall, but didn't have time to read. Or maybe there are two or three books that were Christmas presents that you haven't gotten into yet. But the best answer to this quest is often an old book that you have read many times before, but that keeps coming back to haunt you. Maybe you can get into Tolstoy's *War and Peace* again, or Fitzgerald's *The Great Gatsby* or Steinbeck's *East of Eden*. Books that grab you like that don't come around often, and they make the best companions to visit again on a cold winter's day when the chores are all taken care of, and the crackling fire in the fireplace is beckoning to you.

114

The Sleigh Ride

Several years ago, our family was invited to Libby Lloyd's Airdrie Farm out on the Old Frankfort Pike for the afternoon. There was deep snow on the ground and the temperature was not supposed to go above seven degrees the entire day, but we didn't even consider declining, because we had been invited to come for a ride in her marvelous, enormous sleigh. This was a treat not to be taken lightly.

When we arrived, we saw that the sleigh was large enough to hold more than a dozen people, provided some of these were children. We parents had dressed the little ones in layers of warm clothes, snowsuits, hats, mittens, and boots, and still we worried that they might get cold. We took along heavy wool blankets and earmuffs just in case and ended up glad we had them.

We crowded onto the sleigh, and Carl Lathrem started the motor of the big tractor that was being used to pull us along. His face, nearly frosted over, looked like a true-to-life drawing of Santa Claus. Tommy Roach and Owen Rouse, teenagers who had joined in the great adventure, rode standing up on the back of the sleigh so they could jump off periodically and throw snowballs at each other and at the rest of us. The younger children squealed with delight as the big sleigh bounded over the countryside, and we sang every Christmas carol that we knew.

This exciting ride was twice as special because of the land we were sliding over. That farm is part of the old Woodburn that was purchased in 1790 by Robert Alexander, Libby's direct ancestor. Woodburn's golden age was between 1865 and 1880, when forty-four percent of the nation's top-ranking horses came from that farm, making it the premier horse establishment in America, if not in the world. The great stallion Lexington who stood at Woodburn, was America's leading sire for sixteen years, a record in thoroughbred racing that has not been broken to this very day. This magnificent horse no doubt had cavorted in the same fields we were riding over more than a century later.

On our cold winter's day, we thought about the annual horse sale that took place at Woodburn during Lexington's time. On these very grounds, hundreds of people would be arriving from the train at Spring Station all morning in all kinds of conveyances, on horseback and on foot. Some would be coming from as far away as New York and Texas. Neighbors from all around made their plans early to be here every year. Held in a beautiful grove of bluegrass, the very best annual horse auction in America would begin promptly at ten o'clock and would continue throughout most of the day. The famous Bluegrass caterer, G. Jaubert, was sure to be on hand with enough of his marvelous Kentucky burgoo to feed the multitudes. Other food and drink would be plentiful on great tables placed under the trees, including a generous supply of Old Crow.

As we swirled over the beautiful hills and down the valleys on the big sleigh, we could almost hear the murmurs of laughter of the crowds from those incredible days of yesteryear.

After a long and exciting ride and an invitation to come inside the house for cookies and hot chocolate, we laughingly decided that if Norman Rockwell could have gone on this sleigh ride with us, there was a good chance we would have been on the cover of next year's Christmas edition of *The Saturday Evening Post*.

Shucks!

Windy Sharon is a good man, a master builder, a loyal Baptist, a devoted friend, and a loving husband, father and grandfather. His family is the most important thing in the world to him, and he tries to spend as much time as possible with them. He lives in Midway on Spring Station Road, just before you get to the Midway Cemetery, and keeps his yard as neat as a pin. He also has a wonderful sense of humor and had a good laugh when he told about his grandson Mason.

It seems that the ladies of the family wanted to go shopping shortly before Christmas, and Windy agreed to keep his grandson if Mason would come to his house until his mother could get back from Lexington. When it was time for the boy to get his bath, Windy sat on the edge of the tub in the bathroom, running the water for him. The four-year-old child undressed in the other room and came walking down the hallway without any clothes on. As he approached the bathroom, he had to walk by a full-length mirror. As he passed it, his eyes opened wide, and he turned and walked back until he was standing directly in front of the mirror. It was the first time he had ever seen himself in his entirety. Windy could not possibly guess what was going through the child's mind, so he sat waiting quietly.

SHUCKS!

Mason looked up and down at his reflection several times and then said with a voice full of surprise and disappointment, "Shucks! I'm fat!!"

From the time this story began circulating around Midway, Mason's honest declaration has become catchwords for many of us every time we pass by a mirror on the wall.

"Who Did What?"

For many many years the game of bridge was the most popular form of entertainment for many Midway residents. Often in the 1950s and 1960s, four ladies would get together and play twice a month for nickels and dimes. This bridge would be played in the home of one of the players if she still had children under foot, so a sitter would not be needed. The three guests would bring their own sandwiches and chips and the hostess would provide the soft drinks. Each week they changed partners, and substitutes were arranged if any one of the four had to miss – which they rarely did.

Also on Sunday nights, two couples would get together to play two or three rounds. These were just for amusement, although sometimes players would take the game very seriously and play for blood.

But the round robin bridge games were the most anticipated. About twenty-four people would get together for bridge after a light supper. (Food was not the main attraction for these gatherings.) You would be assigned a seat at one of the six tables and would move at the appropriate time to another seat at the next table. You never knew who your partner would be or how he/she played the game. These contests would last until the wee small hours of the morning, and the prize would be some trinket that had been picked up by the hostess that morning. The real prize would be basking in the glory of being the best bridge player in the house that particular evening, as most of the players there were highly competitive.

There were a couple of men in the group who came along just to make up the correct number at the tables, as their wives loved to play the game. These men had a hard time keeping their level of interest up and after a round or two of bidding at their tables, they were frequently heard to say, "Now, who did what?" Someone finally found cocktail napkins for one of these events that had a bridge logo on them with a man asking that very question.

One evening, most of the local best players were in attendance at a five-table competition, which was being played in a basement family room large enough to accommodate all the tables. Dick and Hilda Starks brought new cards for one table as the hostess had just enough for four. These new cards were waiting on a table where four of the best players of the area happened to sit down to play. It was only after playing for over an hour that Ruth Roach finally stated that the deck at the table "didn't shuffle thick enough." Could some cards be missing? Dick and Hilda burst out laughing and admitted that Dick had slit the cellophane wrappers of the new cards with his pocketknife, removed the deuce of each suit and carefully put the rest of the cards back in the box. He then slid the box back into the cellophane, and no one had noticed the slit. He was trying to play a joke on the hostess, because he "owed her one," but the joke turned out to be on the serious bridge players who had not discovered the deception even after an hour's play. They never were allowed to live this down.

Winter Nights

A great number of our friends who live in Woodford County go to Florida in the winter because they hate the Kentucky cold and the ice on the roads, and because it is a tradition that has been handed down by their families for generations. It is true they miss the complication that winter weather consistently brings. But on the other hand, they also miss the winter fires, the snow falling (making the town look like one of those balls that you hold in your hand and shake until the falling snow comes over the church steeple), and the chili suppers.

For the folks that stay at home, it isn't hard to find friends who are eager to come over for an evening of chili, gossip, listening to music or playing cards. Chili is easy because you go to the basement freezer, get out a package that you froze last summer, made with the tomatoes that you planted down by the back fence. All of a sudden you remember the taste of the tomato that you ate just after you had gathered some in your basket when they were still warm from the sunlight. You didn't even bother to take it inside to add salt to it but stood eating it in the yard just as you picked it. The juice ran down your fingers. The flavor comes back over you, standing at your basement freezer six months later.

WINTER NIGHTS

Preparing the supper is no problem. You cook the thawed chili for the twenty minutes that's needed, adding spaghetti for the last twelve. You make sure you have enough crackers and go to the market to buy a salad ready to serve. You make a platter of brownies, being sure to use the pecans that were a Christmas gift. You bring logs in from the garage and light the fire in the fireplace in the den where you have put up a makeshift table. Supper will be served in here when the friends arrive. You even thought to buy a bunch of daisies at the market to make this a really festive evening. When friends such as Mike and Jennifer Steen come in from the cold evening air, they stand with their backs to the fire warming themselves, waiting for you to pour a glass of red wine to warm them even more. They'll be staying late tonight because they dread the first blast of cold air that will surely greet them when they open the door to start the short walk home across the neighbors' backyards in the glistening, crunchy snow.

O Christmas Tree

Midway is a wonderful place to be during the Christmas season. The shop windows glisten with hundreds of little white lights, and the streets are decorated with beautiful Christmas wreaths. The shops have an open house on one pre-holiday Sunday afternoon, where many serve fancy refreshments. The members of the Lions Club take gift baskets of donated food and toys to the less fortunate, and the children from churches go around the town singing Christmas carols, especially for the aged or shut-ins. Santa used to arrive on the train that would stop beside the little park at City Hall, and he would have treats for all the children who would meet this train. Several years ago, the Womens Club offered prizes for the best decorated front doors in town, and for the best decorated business window. This created a spirited and delightful competition. In the past, there have been walking tours where decorations or interesting historical spots in town were pointed out, and once carols were sung by the walkers as they strolled down the streets.

One of the most meaningful Christmas traditions of Midway is that of taking small gifts that have been handmade around to people that you are thinking about during the holiday time. People make beaten biscuits, candy, bourbon balls, cakes, candles, cookies, decorations, cheese treats and many other goodies which they take around to several doors, usually on Christmas Eve. Mary Jones, a ninety-three-year-old lady, makes red velvet Christmas bows to give to anyone who comes by to visit her during the holidays, and one year she ran out of bows even thought she had made forty-eight.

One of our family customs was to go with Ben Roach to cut our own cedar Christmas tree. Ben would drive an ancient farm truck and we would go very early in the morning of the appointed day. Ben's patients Louis and Valeria Redden live down in Franklin County and they owned a farm that had one field completely filled with cedar trees. Every Christmas they insisted that we come and cut our trees from that field. Ben and Jack would cut a truck load; one for our house, one for his, one for Ben's church and one for his pastor's house. Jack and Ben usually cut several for the church to sell.

The Reddens lived in "Kennebeck Hall" where they ran a foster home for the state, which was located next door to their farm. We stopped to visit them one year while we were getting trees and were impressed with the warm and caring atmosphere in this home. Louis and Valeria had four children of their own and, as I remember it, they kept about twenty other boys and girls there. The big old Hall had one wing for boys and one for girls. These foster children were treated exactly the same as their own and were overwhelmed by the goodness of this couple.

They were certainly generous with their cedars. Choosing a Christmas tree from the great outdoors requires an essential adjustment of size in your mind. The first tree we brought home wouldn't go in the front door until we cut it about in half. Trees in a field look very small and insignificant. Brought into the house it is a different story. I remember one year, the tree was so big that when we got it home we had to remove furniture from the dining room to make space for this huge round ball of a tree that jetted out from the corner to the center of a small room partly under the chandelier. We had to eat all our Christmas meals in the kitchen that year and became a little more careful of size after that.

The best thing about cutting your own cedar tree for Christmas is the marvelous aroma that permeates the entire house once the tree is brought inside. Fir or spruce trees that are beautifully shaped are much easier to decorate – and certainly easier to acquire – but I miss the scent of cedar that means Christmas. I still go into the back yard to cut cedar sprigs to sprinkle over the house before the holidays just for this scent, and that helps but it will never take the place of the old full-fledged cedar aroma of those Christmastimes.

Commitments

Rituals have always played an important time in the social life of Woodford County. Some that were loved, like the May Day at the Girl's School and the Shakertown Bike Ride with its bountiful brunch, have gone by the wayside. However, many remain that enrich our lives.

We still have housewarmings. If you move to a new house or apartment, look out. On an unsuspecting evening, an army of friends will descend bearing food, drink, presents, and endless good will. Usually the "guests" will stay to clean up and when the last one departs, there is no way to tell except for the memories.

Pancake Day at election time has continued as a tradition in Midway for decades. After you vote in May or November, you can wander over to the Christian Church building any time of day for pancakes made from Weisenberger Mill's mix and served with syrup, sausages and coffee. Usually, you will find a hot discussion on the politics of the day as well.

"Railroad Days" weekend rolls around every September, sponsored by the Merchants of Midway. The town braces for a delightful onslaught of tourists who bolster the local economy while having a wonderful time. On every street in town there will be parked cars that brought people for crafts, food, pony rides, live music, and dancing in the streets. It is a lot of hard work for the merchants, great fun for the visitors.

Birthdays are traditionally not forgotten in Woodford County. Friends are very much on hand to help you celebrate whether you want to or not. Hilda Starks, Bett Weisenberger, and I took each other to lunch on birthdays for over twenty years until Hilda's death in November of 1996. We two have continued the custom, but we miss Hilda. Toss Chandler, Jennifer Steen, and I have also begun this practice and it is wonderful to be remembered twice on your special day.

There are a good many locals who celebrate their birthdays under the sign of Leo. Besides myself, there are Betty Ann Voigt, Margaret Ware Parrish, Mary Jones, and Ben Chandler. We do different things with each of these people every summer just to celebrate the fact that we're "still here." Mary's celebration of her ninety-third will guarantee a truckload of cards from Woodford Countians who wish her well.

Another annual birthday celebration is held for Pat Davis whose birthday falls in between Christmas and New Year's Day. This cause gives Bett Weisenberger, Connie Clinkenbeard, Lily May Clark, Mary Howell Davis, Joni Hagan, and me a day to prop up our feet and enjoy each other's company. We take shelter on this day from the stress of the holidays by just talking and relaxing with Pat and this seems to restore us in body and spirit.

Jack and I have celebrated birthdays with our Versailles friends Wendell and Ann Harris and Pat and "B" Williams for over twenty-five years, and we're still counting. The six of us have gotten together for each of the birthdays and for Christmas ever since we decided to give a wine tasting party together when we barely knew each other. One time we drove to Casey County to commemorate Jack's birthday. We drove all that distance because the owner of the Village Restaurant was willing to bake a banana pudding fresh for him that morning for breakfast.

These traditions that we practice every year mark much more than the passage of time and our lives. They also delineate the commitment of friendship and caring that runs deep within the people of this community. This commitment is even more extraordinary than the incredible beauty of this place called Woodford County.

Acknowledgements

My heartfelt thanks to every friend who offered enthusiastic support and encouragement towards this project. Several people even phoned unsolicited to remind me of something wonderful that had occurred years ago, and these contributions are truly gratifying.

In particular, I would like to thank Maxine Gilkinson, Mary Ann McCauley, Libby Raisor Kelly, Steele Davis, Margaret Ware Parrish, Ben Roach, Nelson Prewitt, Warren Mitchell, Guwynn Campbell, Rex Cecil, Les Duncan, Brereton Jones, Bill Clark, Phil Weisenberger, Joe Garrett, Roberta House, Ida Lee Craig, and Chuck Bradley for their contributions and interest.

Kerr's History of Kentucky, Volume III; *If These Walls Could Talk* by Margaret Ware Parrish; and *Woodford County: The First Two Hundred Years*, edited by Margaret Ware Parrish and Dabney Garrett Munson were helpful resources, as were the Woodford County Court Records.

The Archives at the Woodford County Historical Society were invaluable, particularly the tapes of the past copies of *The Woodford Sun*.

ACKNOWLEDGEMENTS

My gratitude extends especially to Jack Fisher for his constancy and encouragement throughout the writing of this book, and his red-pencil help during the past year. Also, I'm grateful to Margaret Ware Parrish, Donna Allen, Jennifer Steen, Toss Chandler, Joe Garrett, and Phil Weisenberger for their willingness to proofread, to Dobree Adams for the final editing of this manuscript, and to Jonathan Greene of Gnomon Press for the original design and production.

About the Author

Jonelle Jones Fisher, author of *Ahead of the Hounds*, was born in Lyon County, Kentucky, in the summer of 1933. She moved with her family to Louisville when she was twelve years old and graduated from the University of Louisville in 1954. She and her husband, Dr. Jack Fisher married in 1956 just after his sophomore year in medical school. When his training was completed, they moved with their two children to the small town of Midway, Kentucky where he began his practice of General Medicine. They are still very much a vital part of the fabric of the community.